Secrets

of the WITCH

To all the women in our lives, and to
our wonderful editor Chloe
J. L. & E. W.

Brimming with creative inspiration, how-to projects, and useful information to enrich your everyday life, Quarto Knows is a favorite destination for those pursuing their interests and passions. Visit our site and dig deeper with our books into your area of interest: Quarto Creates, Quarto Cooks, Quarto Homes, Quarto Lives, Quarto Drives, Quarto Explores, Quarto Gifts, or Quarto Kids.

Secrets of the Witch © 2020 Quarto Publishing plc.
Text by Julie Légère and Elsa Whyte
Illustrations by Laura Pérez

First Published in 2020 by Wide Eyed Editions, an imprint of The Quarto Group.
100 Cummings Center, Suite 265D, Beverly, MA 01915, USA.
T (1)978 282 9590 F (1)978 283 2742 **www.QuartoKnows.com**

First published in France under the title:
Secrets de Sorcières: Une initiation à notre histoire et nos savoirs
©2019, De La Martinière Jeunesse, 57 rue Gaston Tessier, 75019 Paris
www.lamartinierejeunesse.fr

A catalog record for this book is available from the British Library.

ISBN 978-0-7112-5799-3

The illustrations were created digitally
Set in Scala and Gaudy

Published by Georgia Amson-Bradshaw
Edited by Lucy Brownridge
Translated by Lili Owen-Rowlands
Designed by Sasha Moxon
Production by Dawn Cameron

Manufactured in Guangdong, China TT112020
9 8 7 6 5 4 3 2

MIX
Paper from responsible sources
FSC® C016973

JULIE LÉGÈRE   ELSA WHYTE   LAURA PÉREZ

Secrets
of the WITCH

AN INITIATION INTO OUR
HISTORY AND WISDOM

WIDE EYED EDITIONS

"To be a witch is to break the law and invent a whole new one."
Thérèse Clerc in the film
Witches, My Sisters (2010)

"We are the granddaughters of the witches you couldn't burn."
Feminist saying

Contents

Dear sister,

If this book has found its way into your possession, then it means it is time for you to begin your apprenticeship. No doubt you've already sensed some of your powers; this manual will help you to develop them, for without knowledge, power is nothing. These pages will explain all you need to know about us and what went before us.

History has rarely been kind to witches. Although there are stories of good fairies, "white" magic, and benevolent and protective forces, we are almost always associated with "black" or evil magic and a desire to cause harm. Many people believe witches are old women with hooked noses and pointed hats. They believe we concoct horrible potions in cauldrons to curse people whom we are jealous of. Some say that we ride broomsticks by moonlight and worship the devil! They would have you believe that we live on the edge of society, in huts in the depths of the forest, and if we appear young or beautiful, it is only a spell to hide our true selves.

But this is not our story. The time has come to retell and reclaim our identity. Are you ready to discover who we really are?

Etymology

The word "sorcerer" has its roots in the Latin word *"sors,"* which means "fate." A sorceress is a person who has the ability to change the fate of another.

The word "magic" is even older. It comes from the Persian word *"magus,"* which means science and wisdom.

Witches
AND FOLKLORE
around the world

Baba Yaga
Eastern Europe and Russia

In Slavic mythology, Baba Yaga is an old woman with wild hair who guards the entrance to hell. It is said that her mouth can stretch from the ground to the gates of hell and that she uses it to devour travelers who pass her. Famed for her great wisdom and knowledge, she uses them to help those whom she believes to be worthy and pure. She lives deep in the forest in a wooden house that stands on chicken legs. The gate that surrounds her house is made from the bones of the dead.

The Befana
Italy

The Befana is often unkindly described as a badly dressed old woman who is said to fly around on a broomstick. This might make her sound like a traditional storybook witch, but according to Italian folklore, she is kind: at Christmas, she brings gifts to good children and charcoal to naughty ones. This legend dates back to ancient Rome, and when Italy became Catholic, it was rewritten by the Church. The Catholic version says Befana refused to help the Three Kings find the baby Jesus. She later regretted her decision and tried to make up for it by giving out gifts to sleeping children in the hope that one of them might be Jesus.

Yama-Uba
Japan

IN JAPANESE MYTHOLOGY, Yama-Uba is a witch of the mountains. She is an old woman with long white hair who dresses in a distinctive, disheveled red kimono. She also has the power to change her appearance and trick her victims. It is said that her mouth is as wide as her head, and that her hair can transform into snakes. She lives in the depths of the forest, and if a stray traveler crosses her path, she will eat them.

"White" magic versus "black" magic:
A QUESTION OF INTENTION

FOR CENTURIES, people have believed in two types of magic: "white" and "black." Traditionally, "white" magic has been seen as the magic of good—a protective and positive natural magic. One form of "white" magic is Wicca: a modern form of magic founded on the principle that it is immoral to direct magic at a person who is not aware of it. It is forbidden to hurt others. If a Wiccan does hurt another, they are punished by the "law of the triple return," which means they themself will be hurt three times as badly. In contrast, people have believed that "black" magic is evil, dangerous, and bad. It relies on summoning and invoking demons and other evil spirits. However, the distinction between "white" and "black" magic is inaccurate. Magic is magic, and the only difference lies within our intentions and how we choose to use it.

Nature as a Magical FORCE

IN ANCIENT TIMES, religions tended to have many gods. Each god would represent a different force of nature, both good and bad. In ancient Greece, some women were priestesses and oracles who had a special ability to connect with the divine realm and decode the signs sent by the gods on Mount Olympus. But why did these oracles tend to be women? Women were seen to be more closely tied to the Earth and nature, because they gave birth and were the creators of life. In ancient times, it was believed that this special connection to the course of life gave women the power to read the signs in nature and understand the power of plants, crystals, and the planets...

The
MOON

THE MOON is very important to us witches. In Greek mythology, the goddesses Hecate, Artemis, and Selene are all associated with the moon. In contrast, Artemis's male twin, Apollo, is the sun god.

Hecate was the goddess of witchcraft and magic. She reigned over the Earth and the underworld, presiding over each and every spell that was cast.

As well as being the moon goddess, Artemis was the goddess of hunting. During the Middle Ages, people started to call Artemis a "witch" too.

In ancient Greece, a group of witches from a town called Thessaly became notorious. People said they had the power to pull the moon down from the sky, brew dangerous potions, and read the future. This tale continued into ancient Rome, where stories told of a Thessalian witch named Erichtho, who managed to bring a dead soldier back to life.

Guardians OF PLANTS and destinies

DIVINATION AND DESTINY have long been associated with women. In ancient Greece, oracles were called Sibyls. The oracle at Delphi was among the most famous. She was the high priestess of the temple and she was named the Pythia. Oracles read the signs from the gods and told the future. In ancient Rome, the three Parcae, or the three Fates, were women who embodied destiny. They controlled the lives of not just people on Earth, but also the gods.

People's perceptions of women as close to the gods and to Mother Earth led them to believe women understood the healing properties of plants. In ancient myth, the enchantress Medea advises Jason on how to put a dragon to sleep using herbs. This useful and "feminine" skill is something that is shown as being rather suspicious in the story of Medea. The story of Medea and the roles of the Pythia and the Sibyls show how the witch started to take shape in ancient times.

17—

The magic of ancient Egypt

IN ANCIENT EGYPT, magic was everywhere: it maintained the balance of the universe, protected, and healed. Words themselves had magical power, so that to say or write something was to make it live. Knowing the name of a god or enemy gave you power over them, and this was where the notion of "incantations," or spells that were spoken or sung, came from. Amulets with images of gods or magical objects on them were also important. Ancient Egyptians believed that human beings, nature, and the gods were all linked together, as were medicine, magic, and religion. Doctors were said to get their healing powers from the gods. In particular, the powerful goddess Sekhmet was responsible for illnesses, death, and healing, and she was also the patron saint of doctors, who devoted themselves to her.

The druidesses

IN ANCIENT CELTIC SOCIETIES, there were many women druids. These druidesses— or *bandrúi*, as they were known—played an important role in the community, as they possessed knowledge of plants that could be used as protection or medicine. The female druids were also skilled in the art of divination. They can also be found in Celtic mythology and in Breton folklore (from Brittany in France) as the *Gallisenae,* a group of nine druidesses who lived as recluses on the Île de Sein, just off the coast of mainland France. According to legend, they could control winds and storms, deliver prophecies, and transform into animals.

Hermes Trismegistus & correspondence principle

THIS UNUSUAL NAME belongs to an ancient mythical character, the holder of all knowledge. He is associated with two gods: Thoth, the ancient Egyptian god of wisdom, and Hermes, the ancient Greek messenger of the gods and the guider of souls to the underworld. Hermes Trismegistus is credited with writing many of the founding texts of the magical world, including one called the *Emerald Tablet*. He famously stated: "That which is below corresponds to that which is above, and that which is above corresponds to that which is below." He explains that everything in the cosmos is united, from the smallest to the largest things. Planets, colors, the human body—everything was created from a single source and so works in the same way. To understand one thing is to understand another. This was his "principle of correspondence," and it became the basis of magic: everything is linked and the universe is a living entity that is governed by intertwining forces. His writings also relate to alchemy (see p. 23).

Circe

I AM THE DAUGHTER OF PERSE AND HELIOS, THE GREEK GOD OF THE SUN, AND I AM THE HIGH PRIESTESS OF THE GODDESS HECATE. MY POWERS ARE IMMENSE: I CAN TAKE THE STARS FROM THE SKY, CONTROL THE ELEMENTS AND THE ANIMALS, MAKE MYSELF INVISIBLE, AND TRANSFORM MYSELF. I HAVE A DEEP KNOWLEDGE OF PLANTS AND HERBS, AND AM AN EXPERT IN POTION MAKING. NO MAN CONTROLS WHAT I DO, NOR DO THEY DARE TO CROSS MY PATH. WHEN ODYSSEUS INVADED MY ISLAND OF AEAEA, I PROVED MY POWERS BY TURNING THE REST OF HIS CREW INTO PIGS!

The
MIDDLE AGES
and the distrust of magic

MAGIC IS NEITHER GOOD NOR EVIL—it is what is done with it that determines its value. First and foremost, magic is made up of a harmonious link with nature, a way of seeing the world and the forces that rule it. Yet, over the ten centuries that form the Middle Ages, our rituals and practices began to be judged, misunderstood, and eventually associated with the devil, resulting in magic being seen as the embodiment of absolute evil in the Christian religion. "Magic" had now become "witchcraft." Unfortunately, we were now thought of as dangerous beings, and the laws that were written during this time would serve as the basis of our persecution over the coming centuries...

Seizing the SACRED

IN EUROPE, pagan religions and cults that worshipped many gods (polytheistic) were replaced by religions with only one God (monotheistic). By the 5th century, Christianity had become the largest religion. Gradually, the traditions of pagan cults were dropped or changed to fit the new, more popular religion. For example, our knowledge of herbs and our relationship to the moon were reduced to superstitions, seen as false and irrational beliefs that must be banished. From then on, only Christian rituals were considered sacred.

In 506 CE, it was decided during the Council of Agde that augurs (the priests of ancient Rome) and those who consulted them would be outcast, considered "strangers to the Church." In the 7th century, Bishop Isidore of Seville went even further. In his attempts to get rid of magic, he said that it had been taught to humans by demons. This myth would prove fatal to our kind for many centuries.

But the church's original aim was to reeducate those who believed in the witches, so that they might find God. In 906, the church's approach to witches was fixed in writing for the first time in a text called the canon *Episcopi*. It cemented the idea that magic was evil and the work of women. By the 13th century, the Church saw us as an urgent and real danger.

"EVEN NOW, THERE ARE CERTAIN WICKED WOMEN WHO, MISLED BY THE WILES AND TRICKS OF THE DEVIL, BELIEVE AND DECLARE THAT IN THE NOCTURNAL HOURS, WITH DIANA, THE GODDESS OF THE HEATHEN (...). IF ONLY THESE WOMEN HAD BEEN THE ONES TO DIE IN THEIR TREACHERY AND HAD NOT DRAGGED MANY OTHER PEOPLE WITH THEM INTO THE VIOLENT AND UNTIMELY DEATH OF FAITHLESSNESS!"

Canon Episcopi, 906

Magic of the people

IN THE COUNTRYSIDE, pagan practices and beliefs were now called superstitions in order to make Christian practices seem more important. However, certain magic practices—such as alchemy and astrology were spared. They were considered to be more established and academic because they had come from the first writings about magic translated from Arabic. Often used by well-educated and privileged men, these forms of magic were associated with the powerful and therefore tolerated by the Church. In contrast, we witches and wizards saw our knowledge trampled on because it was considered to be the magic of the people, not the powerful.

Alchemy

AN ANCIENT DISCIPLINE, alchemy blends science, philosophy, and religion, and is based on the idea that everything, from the smallest element to the largest, is intimately linked. The idea comes from the teachings of Hermes Trismegistus (see p. 19), whose texts were written in a mysterious language only understood by a few people. The gold of alchemy is related to the sun, while silver is linked to the moon, and copper to Venus. Alchemists aimed to transform matter using an "alembic," a scientific instrument used to separate the elements by heating and cooling them. Alchemists had two goals: the first was the making of "the philosopher's stone," a stone able to transform lead (considered an imperfect metal, because water, air, and fire tarnish it) into gold, and the second was the creation of the Panacea, an elixir that could make life longer or even help to obtain eternal youth.

Magic BECOMES witchcraft

FROM THE 8TH CENTURY, the Church officially recognized that witchcraft was not just superstition, but a dangerous practice. In the 1233 decree *Vox in Rama*, Pope Gregory IX proclaimed the existence of secret ceremonies taking place under the influence of the devil. This was an unfortunate development that foreshadowed what would come later...Magic, pagan beliefs were now only talked about as witchcraft and the worship of evil; good and bad stood in opposition to one another. There wasn't much understanding of science at the time, so good things that happened were called miracles and were believed to be the work of God. Anything bad and unexplained was blamed on witchcraft. The pagan traditions of the countryside were completely demonized. The Catholic philosopher Thomas Aquinas wrote that plant remedies were useless and really the work of demons.

In 1326, Pope John XXII wrote *Super Illius Specula,* in which he said witchcraft was "heresy" (meaning in opposition to Catholic beliefs). Those suspected of taking part in magical practices could now be sentenced by the Inquisition, the court in charge of convicting heretics (people who committed heresy). Pope John XXII had prohibited the practice of magic and all knowledge associated with it. In France, the first "official" trial for witchcraft took place on October 29, 1390, and it condemned to death by burning our sister Jeanne de Brigue in 1931. Witch trials were still rare, but they inspired and gave rise to our worst enemies: the demonologists.

Jeanne
OF BRIGUE

AUGUST 19, 1391

My name is Jeanne, but I am also known as "La Cordelière," meaning a cord or tassel. I learned my gift from my godmother, who taught me all I know. In my region, many people visit me to help them to find objects they have lost or to track down thieves, but I also know how to heal others, too. My powers scare others, and his grace the Bishop of Maux imprisoned me for a year and banned me from practicing magic. But people still knew of me, and when a woman came to ask me to help her son who was ill, what was I supposed to do? Refuse her? This is how I met my dear Macette, who also knows the art of magic. She revealed to me that her husband, Hennequin, used to hurt her, until one day she mixed together wax and resin in a hot pan, while invoking the devil and the gospel three times. This caused Hennequin to feel as though his body were being pricked all over by needles.

I was impressed by Macette's skill, but I convinced her to stop harming Hennequin. We then became friends and I asked her to assist me in making my own potion. My boyfriend, the father of my children, was refusing to marry me, so I wanted to make a potion that would make him propose. I was very poor and my condition intolerable, but I didn't have a chance to put this potion to use, as the news of Hennequin had spread and I was arrested and imprisoned in Paris. Macette was locked up shortly after. I have now been imprisoned for more than a year, although it feels like a century. They call us "witches." It is summer now and the sun heats up the pigs in the market, the air is sweet, and we are soon to be taken to the stake. We will be killed for having been beaten, having helped to heal others, and for wanting to be married. Goodbye, Macette— let us burn!

The
RENAISSANCE
Witch Hunts

MOST PEOPLE THINK that the Renaissance was a time of great progress and renewal, which is true in many ways. Unfortunately, for our sisters, it was a time of darkness. Between the 15th and 17th centuries, tens of thousands of women were killed out of fear. Several books on demonology were published in Europe, which made people terrified of witches. During the Renaissance, witchcraft was officially recognized as a crime punishable by death, which led to persecution by both the Church and the State. As the accusations and lawsuits multiplied, a murderous, frenzied panic spread across Northern Europe.

The turn
OF THE 15ᵀᴴ CENTURY

AT THE DAWN OF THE RENAISSANCE, the Church believed our souls belonged to the devil and that our magic was being conducted in his name. An inquisitor named Heinrich Kramer was convinced that people were ignoring an epidemic of witchcraft raging in Germany. He alerted Pope Innocent VIII, who ordered that cooperation with the Inquisition was compulsory in 1484.

The path was paved for our mortal enemies, the demonologists, who called themselves "specialists in the science of the devil." They led the fight against witchcraft and made new laws that aimed to identify and punish us. Witches were mostly targeted rather than wizards, because everyone assumed that magic was women's business.

In 1486, Kramer published the *Malleus Maleficarum*, or the *Hammer of Witches*, which would influence the two centuries that followed. This manual contained instructions for judges on how to arrest suspected witches and how to conduct their trials. Because of this text, we were cataloged, condemned, and killed as witches.

Demonology

DESPITE THE FACT IT WAS BANNED in 1490 by the Church, copies of the *Malleus Maleficarum* made their way all over Northern Europe. At least 30,000 copies and 30 different editions were printed by the 17th century. Similar pamphlets appeared in its wake, such as *Of the Demon-mania of the Sorcerers* by Jean Bodin in 1580, *Demonolatry* by Nicolas Rémy in 1595, and *An Examen of Witches* by Henry Boguet in 1603.

ALTHOUGH SOME MEN WERE INVESTIGATED, WOMEN WERE THE MAIN VICTIMS OF PERSECUTION, REPRESENTING AROUND 80% OF ACCUSATIONS AND 85% OF CONVICTIONS.

How to HUNT a witch

THE WITCH HUNTERS traveled through Germany tracking suspected witches, with copies of *Malleus Maleficarum* tucked under their arms. The local religious authorities followed the book like an instruction manual. It stated that all you needed to convict a suspect was two statements from different accusers that matched. In some extreme cases, children were encouraged to testify against their own mothers! People began to see signs of witchcraft everywhere: the strange behavior of a neighbor could lead to an accusation of witchcraft. In many cases, these accusations were fueled by personal vendettas.

What happened next to our sisters accused of witchcraft was horriffic. Sisters suspected of being witches. The procedure demanded the accused confess to their crimes so that they could be sentenced. Suspects would be put in prison and would have their heads shaved. They would be searched for marks of the devil—the indisputable proof of their being a witch. Then they were subjected to extreme torture, often even after they had "confessed." They would be given life imprisonment, banishment, or death by hanging, burning at the stake, or even in an oven. Most trials ended with the accused being killed at the stake.

France, Switzerland, and Germany were the countries in which the witch hunters were most brutal. Between the 16th and 17th centuries, during the height of the persecutions, magistrates prided themselves on their cruelty, often boasting how unpleasant they had been. In Germany alone, 30,000 of our sisters were hunted and burned at the stake, which even caused a shortage of firewood. After all the trials were over, there were even some German villages with only one surviving woman each.

"IF THE ACCUSED CONFESSES UNDER TORTURE, THEY MUST REPEAT THE CONFESSION AFTER TWENTY-FOUR HOURS IN A DIFFERENT LOCATION. IF THEY RETRACT THEIR STATEMENT, THEY MUST BE SUBJECTED TO TORTURE ONCE MORE."

An Examen of Witches, 1603

SUDDEN DEATH OF A CHILD AFTER SHE GAVE IT BREAD; BLINDING A MAN, WOMAN, AND TWO CHILDREN; DRYING UP OF A COW'S MILK; DEATH OF A HORSE; ATTEMPTED CHILD KIDNAPPING; ENTERING A HOUSE BY NIGHT IN THE GUISE OF A CAT. *List of the crimes of Adrienne d'Heur, 60 years old, burned to death as a witch on September 11, 1646*

The devil's mark

PEOPLE BELIEVED THAT we had sworn allegiance to the devil and that when we did, he marked us with his clawed hands. And given how the devil is by nature deceitful, these marks could take many difference forms, such as scratches, birthmarks, moles, and warts. And even if at first no mark was found on you, worry not, for the judges would discover one by any means possible...

We were accused of...

BRINGING RAIN, lightning, hail, poisoning the water in wells, spreading the plague, killing babies for food, causing stillbirths, worshipping the devil on a Sunday, causing illnesses of all kinds as a form of revenge on our neighbors, or punishing a man who wanted to be with another woman...

We were suspected if...

WE LIVED ON THE MARGINS OF SOCIETY, we didn't want to get married, we fell in love, we didn't go to church, we went to church too often, our rosary beads were worn out, we moved too often, we had too many boyfriends, we argued with our neighbors, we were rude, we walked alone at night, we failed to heal someone's illness, or, even worse, we did heal someone's illness.

Double, DOUBLE, toil and trouble

HOW DO WE EXPLAIN this wave of hatred and violence that lasted for two centuries and was so intense it led to thousands of deaths? Many say Christianity was the cause, and in particular Protestantism, which was common across Europe at this time. Others blame the government that wanted to control people and stop them from overthrowing power by making them scared of witches. Both the Church and the State wanted to reestablish their power and authority over their people, and the witch hunts were a means to do that. They were also a way to pass on the blame of people's general unhappiness and misery: the devil and his witches became the cause of all society's ills, such as the famines and plagues that ravaged the two centuries, which were in reality caused by poor government, crop damage, and pests.

Moreover, in the field of medicine, many "potions" were actually based on "empiricism," which means on evidence drawn from observations and the senses, which the Church was particularly wary of. And these potions were also treated with suspicion because of their deep connection to nature (and therefore to women), which at the time was considered by philosophers and scientists as a force that needed to be controlled. Our sisters were the victims of this kind of thinking: they were seen as "dangerous" because they challenged the established order and tried to break free of the shackles that sought to keep them in their place.

Older women WHO LIVED Alone

THE WOMEN WHO WERE VICTIMS of the witch hunts tended to resemble one another. A great many of them were older women and unmarried. Often they lived alone, sometimes on the outskirts of society at the edges of towns and forests. You might say they were classic fairy-tale caricatures: the old woman lurking inside her hut in the forest. But what these stories leave out is that with age comes wisdom, and that by living in a secluded hut a woman could gain a great deal of knowledge about plants, herbs, and their curative powers. But medicine was meant to be the realm of men, so women who were skilled in it disturbed the established order and so must be working with the devil.

Wise women AND HEALERS

HISTORICALLY, ACROSS THE WORLD, healers have predominantly been women. Both pregnancy and childbirth were exclusively the domain of women, specifically of midwives, whose knowledge was passed down through the centuries by word of mouth. Midwives' knowledge of birth and the body made them the targets of the Inquisition, which accused them of many evils: "No one does more harm to the Catholic faith than midwives," proclaimed the *Malleus Maleficarum*. At the same time, far from the countryside, women were not allowed to be admitted into medical universities. Paracelsus, a doctor and philosopher of the 16th century who claimed to "have learned everything from witches," declared that the university only served to produce "medical schoolmasters" in place of doctors eager to heal or with any concrete experience.

PLANTS were the basis of many of our medicines. Some dangerous plants when used in small doses could help to cure ailments. But if the dose was even slightly incorrect they could cause hallucinations, breathing difficulties, and dilated pupils...which was often taken as a sign that a person had been possessed by the devil.

The Salem
WITCH TRIALS

IT ALL BEGAN IN 1692 in Massachusetts, in a village named Salem, which had been founded by English settlers who had fled religious persecution back home. But their arrival in the New World was not easy: relations with the Native Americans were strained, the climate was more extreme than they were used to, the political situation was treacherous, and a profound fear of the devil was a main preoccupation. Distrust, envy, and boredom set the stage for the drama that would follow...

One cold day in January, a young woman named Abigail and her cousin Betty fell ill. Their eyes rolled back into their heads, they mumbled in an unknown language, and they appeared to howl at the moon. A doctor was called, but being incapable of finding a cause for the pair's illness, he suggested they might be witches. As soon as the word "witch" was uttered, everything went wrong. Ashamed of this accusation, which their Catholic religion condemned, the young girls named three other women who they claimed were the real witches: Tituba, Sarah Good, and Sarah Osborne. In the days that followed, a dozen other young girls who reported suffering from the same ailments provided names of other "witches" in the community. At first, most of the accused were older women who were widowed, remarried, unhappy, or mistrusted, but soon the girls moved on to naming all those who dared to doubt their accusations. It was even thought that Salem's accusers could recognize witches by touch alone.

During the emergency trials, the defendants had to represent themselves. At the trial of Bridget Bishop, dozens of witnesses came forward: one accused her of having put a curse on his child twelve years earlier; another claimed to have been attacked by Bishop's silhouette at dawn, five or six years earlier. This ghostly appearance was known as "spectral proof," and it sealed the fate of many so-called witches. In the neighboring town of Andover, 72 women were also charged. It was total chaos and the toll was heavy. Hundreds were accused and nearly thirty were sentenced to death.

Transcript from the trial of Bridget Bishop, hanged in Salem on June 10, 1692. The trial lasted one day.

Judge: Why do you seem to act witchcraft before us, by the motion of your body, which seems to have influence upon the afflicted.

Bridget Bishop: I know nothing of it. I am innocent to a witch. I know not what a witch is.

J: How do you know then that you are not a witch?

BB: I do not know what you say.

J: How can you know, you are no witch, and yet not know what a witch is?

BB: I am clear: if I were any such person you should know it.

J: You may threaten, but you can do no more than you are permitted.

BB: I am innocent of a witch.

The Triumph
OF REASON

ACROSS 17TH- AND 18TH-CENTURY EUROPE, the bonfires that burned under the stakes were put out. Medicine was progressing, and death and illness blamed on witchcraft and demons were increasingly explained by doctors. Political power had stabilized and the plague disappeared. As people grew less fearful of the world around them, they stopped needing to use witches as scapegoats. Scientists and philosophers aimed to shed new light on the world using knowledge and reason. This is why we call the 18th century the En*light*enment. The universe was now thought of as a mechanism that could be understood through reason. In this new context, witchcraft was seen as nothing more than a harmless superstition belonging to the darkness of yesteryear. The new sacred tome of the Enlightenment was the Encyclopedia. In it, witchcraft was defined as a "magical, shameful or ridiculous practice, mistakenly attributed by superstition to the power of demons."

Poison, Black Mass, and birthmarks

AS INTEREST IN science and reason increased and witch hunts decreased, people started to become suspicious instead of people with power. The "Affair of the Poisons" (see p. 42) was a major scandal in France when a great number of King Louis XIV's inner circle were accused of poisoning, witchcraft, and holding sinister "Black Masses." In 1682, the king decriminalized sorcery, which ordinary people saw as the king protecting his friends. For centuries, the hatred of women had led to witch hunts, but now things had changed. Of course, witchcraft did not disappear entirely, but it was now considered a harmless pastime of the rich and more often took the shape of palmistry, tarot, and reading the future in a person's birthmark.

From witches to liars

IN ENGLAND, the Witchcraft Act of 1735 made it a crime to claim you or anyone else could practice witchcraft or divination. This meant that a new group of people were put on trial—people who self-identified as having powers, and this included many gypsies. The image of the romantic, strange, and free gypsy woman shares many of the features of the witch, but the main difference being that gypsies were not seen as devil worshippers , but deceivers. Gypsies were not feared but they were stigmatized, and sadly some were put to trial. Anna Göldin was the last woman to be burned at the stake for witchcraft in 1782. We still continued to practice, but discreetly, and far away from big cities.

The Affair of the Poisons

IN 1672, A STRANGE SET OF EVENTS shook up high society. A French army captain was found to be in possession of several vials of poison as well as some letters in which his girlfriend, a marquise, admitted to poisoning three people. A few years later, the case was referred to the special court known in France as *la chambre ardente*, or "the burning chamber," which dealt with state crimes. It seemed this was one of many such crimes by different members of the royal court who were very close to King Louis XIV. One of the king's favorites, Madame de Montespan, was even said to have poisoned her rival. The smoldering embers of the witch hunts seemed to have been rekindled in the minds of the people, and the security of the royals was now uncertain. However, although more than 400 suspects were interrogated at trial, most of the senior courtiers were let off. Those found guilty were sent into exile, while non-aristocratic people found guilty of the same crimes were executed. In 1709, the king himself ordered that the records of the whole affair be destroyed.

Catherine Deshayes, THE FORTUNE-TELLER

THIS NIGHT OF FEBRUARY IN 1680, I will burn at the stake at Place de Grève in Paris. I was sentenced and did not challenge it, even if it was largely the fault of the women of the court like Madame de Montespan who demanded my services, but who were protected by their status. I'm not saying it was all their fault, as that would be a lie; indeed, I was very talented at making poisons and providing magical services. It was my fellow poisoners and fortune-tellers Marie Vigoreaux and Marie Bosse who denounced me to the authorities. I performed conjurations, organized Black Masses, and poisoned rivals for big sums of money. But the scandal had to hit within the court in order that Louis XIV be toppled. I provided the authorities with some of the names of my clients, some of whom no doubt shocked the king! Such a shame that it has all come to an end.

Romanticism &
RE-ENCHANTMENT

HAVING BEEN LARGELY IGNORED during the 18th century, gradually, people started to talk about us again. Dry reason and the Enlightenment were slowly being overshadowed by a renewed interest in emotion, adventure, and enchantment. The 19th century would be one rued by feelings, imagination, romance and anguish, dazzling nature and the darkness of night, shadows, mystery and monsters. Science was not abandoned, but as people learned more, they realized just how much was still unknown and yet to be understood. The discovery of X-rays, for example, revealed for the first time what had been invisible within us. Strangely it meant that many people wonder what else might be hidden which awakened belief in the supernatural. Folk stories full of magical beings were dusted off after centuries of contempt. Demons and witches found their way into music, painting, and literature once again.

Witches and fairy tales

THE MOST OBVIOUS EXAMPLE of our welcome back into the arts was in Jules Michelet's essay *Satanism and Witchcraft* from 1862. After over a hundred years, he was the first to look at the hunts we had fallen victims to, and among the first to recognize our sisters' suffering and those who died in vain. He told the stories of independent women who lived alone at the margins and who were excluded from society for enjoying freedom.

In Germany, the Brothers Grimm wrote down the fairy tales from the countryside that had been kept alive through word of mouth. These stories fixated on an image of us as ugly, jealous, and evil old women who lived alone, far away from everything. In these tales, we were the opposite of the beautiful, young, passive, and innocent princesses who could only wait to marry a handsome prince and so live "happily ever after."

"I SHOULD HAVE CONFINED MY AMUSEMENT TO LEARNING SUCH SECRETS FOR THE CURE OF THE HUMAN BODY AS MY GRANDMOTHER TEACHES ME. FLOWERS, HERBS, STONES, INSECTS,—ALL THE SECRETS OF NATURE WOULD HAVE FURNISHED ME WITH ENOUGH OCCUPATION AND PLEASURE AS I LOVE TO ROAM ABOUT AND EXAMINE EVERYTHING, I MIGHT HAVE BEEN ALONE ALL THE TIME WITHOUT KNOWING WHAT IT IS TO BE BORED; FOR MY GREATEST PLEASURE IS TO GO OFF TO THOSE SPOTS WHICH NOBODY KNOWS, AND TO SPEND MY TIME THERE IN DREAMING OF FIFTY THINGS WHICH I HAVE NEVER EVEN HEARD MENTIONED BY PEOPLE WHO THINK THEMSELVES VERY WISE AND THOUGHTFUL.'
George Sand,
Little Fadette, 1849

Voodoo

MEANWHILE, IN THE UNITED STATES, Marie Laveau (see p. 49) was practicing a new form of witchcraft that blended Christianity and the ancient practice of voodoo, as imported by West African former slaves.

Voodoo was a culture, philosophy, and religion that came from 17th-century slave communities who had been brought by force to the Caribbean, Brazil, and the southern United States. Their right to practice their own religion and celebrate their own cultural heritage was denied, including voodoo—a mixture of Yoruba, Fon, and Ewe rites. The Catholic saints were then added to the voodoo deities, which represented natural powers and elements, and over which Mawu, the creator goddess, ruled. This is another form of magic, quite distinct from brooms and cauldrons.

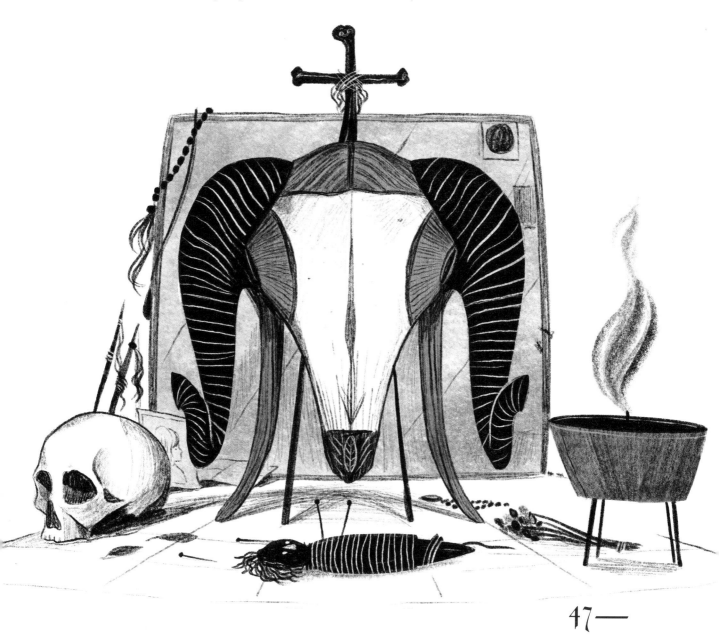

> "WHEN INSTEAD OF 'WITCHES,' WE READ 'WOMEN,' WE GAIN A FULLER COMPREHENSION OF THE CRUELTIES INFLICTED BY THE CHURCH UPON THIS PORTION OF HUMANITY."
>
> Matilda Joslyn Gage, *Woman, Church and State*, 1893

Matilda Joslyn Gage

FOR AS LONG AS I CAN REMEMBER, the injustices of my time have revolted me. I have always refused to accept the place that society holds for women. The laws of the United States only protect rich, privileged men at the expense of everyone else's dignity. I want to make sure these laws change, even if it means breaking them. I have been put in prison for helping black slaves to escape their slave owners. And what is to be done about the status of First Nations citizens, from whom we stole everything? And for what absurd reason are women not allowed to vote?

By campaigning and writing, I demand the abolition of slavery, votes for women, and total equality of all peoples. In my book ***Woman, Church, and State***, I was among the first to describe the abuse of people in the United States during the witch hunts. No one suffered more during this period than women.

Marie Laveau

IN MY CITY, New Orleans, and even beyond the borders of Louisiana, they call me the Voodoo Queen. I am a high voodoo priestess, or mambo—and the most powerful in the New World. I keep a snake named Zombi, who assists me in rituals and ceremonies including divination, hypnosis, bewitchments, and the creation of potions and talismans. My magic is both feared and sought after. But no one would ever dare call me a "witch," for I am a fearsome magician, a priestess worshipped by worshippers, but also a businesswoman, a free woman, and scholar. I have styled the hair of high-society women for decades, provided them with potions and amulets, and created quite a loyal following and reputation. I use voodoo to help and protect, and in particular I fight against public executions, using my magic to soften the sentence for those convicted. I care for bodies as much as for minds. My ancestors taught me how to use plants and make remedies to cure sick people who suffer from yellow fever and cholera.

The Witches RETURN

IN THE 20TH CENTURY, WE STARTED TO BE HEARD. The witch became a symbol of the feminist struggles of the 1970s. Magical practices were tinged with the messages of activism. We called for women's rights, equality for all, and the preservation of our world. Even though we were now accepted, the witch hunts of the past remained one of the least studied areas in history. Through the writings of Silvia Federici, Deirdre English, Barbara Ehrenreich, Starhawk, and Mona Chollet, the gaps in our stories started to be filled and the voices of our ancient sisters grew louder.

Proud TO BE a witch

AT THE BEGINNING OF THE 20TH CENTURY, the dancer Mary Wigman choreographed the first solo created by and for a woman in a piece known as "Witch Dance," while the Argentinian Surrealist artist Leonor Fini drew a whole string of them perched on brooms. In the 1970s, feminist movements rid the word "witch" of its negative associations. People began instead to celebrate us for the freedom and independence that we symbolize. In France in 1975, the journalist Xavière Gautier founded a literary and artistic feminist magazine that she called *Sorcières* (*Witches*). And in the United States, on Halloween 1968, the Women's International Terrorist Conspiracy from Hell, or W.I.T.C.H., armed with cauldrons and pointed hats, cast a spell on the New York Stock Exchange and the next day the stock market reportedly dropped five points. These feminist campaign groups protested against a violent and capitalist society that was run by, and for the benefit of, white men. Even today, "Witch Blocs" still exist in activist circles and during demonstrations the women parade dressed as witches, performing rituals aimed at bringing down all forms of oppression and exclusion.

Witch hunts now

THE EXPRESSION "WITCH HUNT" no longer refers only to those that saw our sisters lose their lives, but also describes the attempt to hunt down and persecute people who have been made into scapegoats. But even the old types of hunts still exist in some regions across the world. Saudi Arabia, for example, has a religious anti-witch police force and witchcraft still figures as a crime punishable by death. In some Indian villages, women who are said to be witches are persecuted and murdered, but accusing someone of practicing witchcraft is punishable by the law. In Ghana, "witch camps" exist for hundreds of women who are forced from their communities following accusations of witchcraft. Deprived of the right to defend themselves, the victims are often widows, sometimes single, and are often accused without proof of causing the deaths of loved ones, of poor harvests, or even of not having given birth to a boy. Across centuries and continents, fear and superstition combine with envy and result in women being blamed and hurt.

"WITCHES HAVE ALWAYS BEEN WOMEN WHO DARED TO BE: GROOVY, COURAGEOUS, AGGRESSIVE, INTELLIGENT, NONCONFORMIST, EXPLORATIVE, CURIOUS, INDEPENDENT, REVOLUTIONARY... YOU ARE A WITCH BY BEING FEMALE, UNTAMED, ANGRY, JOYOUS AND IMMORTAL."
From the W.I.T.C.H. protest group's manifesto

"TREMATE, TREMATE, LE STREGHE SON TORNATE!" "TREMBLE, TREMBLE, THE WITCHES HAVE RETURNED!"
Italian feminist slogan

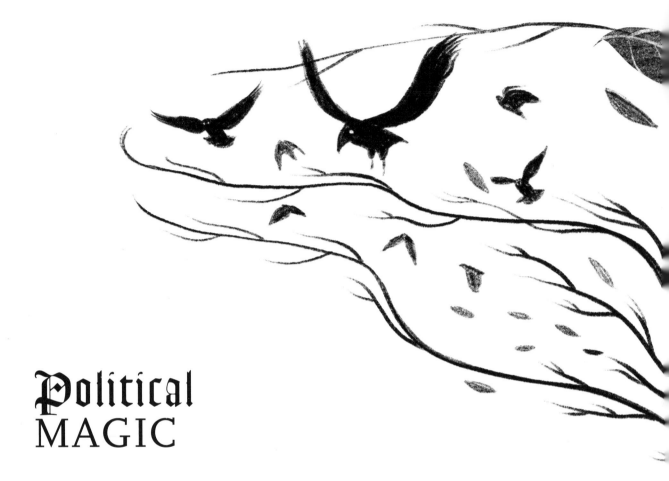

Political MAGIC

AT THE END OF THE 20TH CENTURY, we were seen once again as being in tune with nature. There was a rise in something called "neo-paganism." It brought together strands of Wicca, a modern, nature-based religious movement. Particularly popular among North American feminist communities, Wicca has a strong ecological dimension as it advocates for the protection of the Earth. As the eco-feminist Starhawk writes, "If we cannot dream of the world we want, we cannot create it. It is about restoring and protecting ecological, but also social, political, economic, and cultural ecosystems." A follower of Wicca, Starhawk is a writer, feminist, and anti-capitalist activist, who wants to see more sustainable farming. With imagination and sensitivity, she combines feminism and ecology around a spiritual practice, to encourage harmony between humans and nature.

"MODERN PHYSICS NO
LONGER SPEAKS OF SEPARATE,
DISCRETE ATOMS OF DEAD
MATTER, BUT OF WAVES OF
ENERGY, PROBABILITIES,
PATTERNS THAT CHANGE
AS THEY ARE OBSERVED; IT
RECOGNIZES WHAT SHAMANS
AND WITCHES HAVE ALWAYS
KNOWN: THAT MATTER AND
ENERGY ARE NOT SEPARATE
FORCES, BUT DIFFERENT
FORCES OF THE SAME
THING."
Starhawk

"THE SMOKE OF THE
BURNED WITCHES STILL
HANGS IN OUR NOSTRILS."
Starhawk

Witches in POP CULTURE

IN 1939, THE FILM ADAPTATION OF *The Wizard of Oz* showed a "good witch" on screen for the first time, with the character of Glinda. Later, in the 1960s, there was also the popular television series *Bewitched*, which starred Elizabeth Montgomery as a witch living in present-day America. In the mid-1990s, pop culture became truly obsessed with witches! *Charmed*, *Buffy the Vampire Slayer*, and *Sabrina* all centred around young witches with incredible powers. Above all, these TV series overturned horror film clichés where women and girls tended to be passive victims. At the same time, the novels and film versions of the *Harry Potter* series presented even more positive examples of young women as witches, most notably Hermione Granger. Witches were no longer portrayed as monstrous old women, but strong characters with complex identities, and the desire and ability to fight against injustice.

Hermione Granger & WILLOW ROSENBERG

THE NAME HERMIONE comes from Hermes, the messenger of the gods and the father of alchemy, while the willow is a sacred tree with many special powers. There are many similarities that draw together the characters Hermione from the *Harry Potter* series and Willow from *Buffy the Vampire Slayer*.

INTELLIGENT AND CURIOUS
Both girls are brilliant students who love books and value knowledge.

LOYAL
They would both risk their own lives to help their friends.

REBELLIOUS
Both are sensible and wise beyond their years, but neither would hesitate to break the rules if they considered them to be unfair, or if justice required it.

JUSTICE SEEKERS
They both hate injustices, and see people for who they truly are, without prejudice.

CARING AND PASSIONATE
Hermione goes head-to-head in the battles, always taking the side of the House Elves or those they call "half-bloods," while Willow would do anything for her beloved, Tara. So while neither Hermione nor Willow are the lead characters, both are so essential, they are sometimes considered the true heroines of their respective universes.

Magical SYMBOLS

MAGICAL CUSTOMS are shrouded in mystery, and only shared with a small number of carefully chosen insiders. Your curiosity and your thirst for knowledge make you worthy of these secrets. The passages that follow should help you to lift a section of the veil that covers our world.

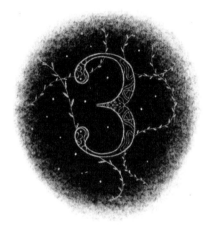

The number three

Past, present, future. Mind, body, soul. Earth, water, sky. Animal, vegetable, mineral. The number three carries great symbolic power in every culture in the world. Like the triangle with which it is associated, the number three represents perfect harmony.

The number seven

The seven wonders of the world, the seven deadly sins, the seven factors of Buddhist awakening, the seven gates of hell, and the seven colors of the rainbow. Seven is one of the most symbolically rich numbers, no doubt because of its association with what astronomers once identified as "the seven stars" and because the lunar phase, as used in ancient Egypt as a calender, lasts for seven days.

The number thirteen

Unlucky for some! Since antiquity, the number thirteen has had a bad reputation. This is most likely because it has the misfortune of coming after twelve, a number historically used as a base figure for counting (instead of ten). From this base figure we have the twelve months of the year, twelve hours of day and night, the twelve signs of the zodiac, the twelve Olympian gods, the twelve labors of Hercules, and even the twelve apostles. Thirteen is also the sacred number of the Mayan people and although the thirteenth card in the tarot represents death, it also symbolizes new beginnings.

Abracadabra

The precise origin of this magical term is unknown, but it's likely that it derives from the Aramaic *adhadda kedhabhra* meaning "let it be destroyed." It is a very old phrase, and the first written recording of the term dates back to the 11th century. To protect from or cure a disease, one would write or engrave this word onto a piece of paper, each time cutting off the last letter to form an inverted triangle.

The Theban alphabet

Published for the first time in 1531, the Theban alphabet was used to record charms and to indicate if something, such as an amulet or talisman, was a magical object. It was also a cipher language used to encode the secret spells and written incantations found in a Book of Shadows (see below).

The Book of Shadows

Every witch has their own Book of Shadows, which contains charms, spells, potions, and magical recipes, as well as notes, observations, and thoughts. It can be written in code using the Theban alphabet, but the main thing is that the notebook bears your magic name. To discover your own, start by clearing your mind. Once your thoughts are settled, grab a felt-tip pen and draw letters at random, keeping your eyes closed. You may need to try several times to find the name that works for you. Then, all you have to do is encode it using the alphabet.

Runes

In the Celtic and Germanic languages, the word rune means "secret," "mystery," or even "knowledge." The inscriptions in this alphabet are usually short and engraved in natural materials such as stone or wood. Each rune represents an element or a concept, and they are used to read the future.

The black cat

Nocturnal, high-minded and solitary, the cat is a sacred animal in Egyptian mythology, associated with the goddess Bastet and the ancient Greek goddess Artemis. During the witch hunts, cats (especially black ones) were burned alongside their owners. Accused of transmitting diseases, many cats were tracked down, in the same way that we were. Sometimes, the discovery of a tuft of white hair, considered to be the finger of God (a reverse mark of the devil), meant the animal was spared.

The owl

For centuries, superstition has dictated that an owl figure, when nailed to a door, can ward off bad luck. But the owl also has a spooky reputation, probably because they fly and hunt by night. Owls have been seen as wise and as bringers of prophecy, but also as omens of death. The similarity of the Latin words *strix*, meaning an owl-like demon, and *striga*, meaning witch or vampire, are another source of the owl's association with "evil."

The bat

The bat looks like a hybrid animal: half mouse and half bird, half earthly and half heavenly. It has been said that its leathery wings are made from the souls of the damned. The bat's love of the nighttime and its jerky flying motion have forever cast it as a shady character in films and stories.

The toad

The toad's saliva is a famous ingredient in making magical potions, but it is very dangerous, so be warned never to touch it. Typically nocturnal, the toad has a viscous, greenish appearance that repulses many. Its significance to witchcraft meant that the breeding of toads was considered a crime that many of us "confessed" to during the Renaissance witch hunts.

The spider

Associated with shadows and darkness, the much-feared spider is often associated with women due to its weaving skills. In turn, the spider's web evokes both fate and the deceptive nature of appearances...

The grimoire

From the Old French term *grammaire*, which was used in the Middle Ages to refer to those books written in Latin, a grimoire is a book of spells. Among the many mysterious grimoires that have been unearthed, a certain number are particularly treasured, including *Clavicula Salomonis*, *Grand Albert*, and *Petit Albert*.

The pointed hat

Although black pointed hats are not quite as old as some of the other images associated with us, their origin is important. Many of our sisters who were victims of the Inquisition were forced to wear headdresses during their interrogations as a means of humiliation. The shape also resembles the hats that Jewish people were forced to wear in certain regions during the Middle Ages as a means of marking them out.

The wand

The wand is a very ancient symbol of magic and clairvoyance (being able to see things not perceived by the senses). The caduceus, a wand surrounded by two snakes, is associated with Hermes and Asclepius, the Greco-Roman gods of medicine. In *The Odyssey*, Circe (see p. 19) waved a wand to cast her spells. Among the Celts, druids and druidesses used wands, which symbolize the influence they had over the elements. Wands are often made of hazel, a tree considered to have magical properties because its roots plunge deep underground and so unite it with the underworld.

The broomstick

At first sight an everyday object, the broomstick escapes domesticity once it is in the air, where it offers unparalleled freedom to those who ride it. A symbol of the home and of the chores typically left to women, the broomstick had a very different significance in ancient times where it was used to preserve the purity of temples and shrines. According to Breton superstition, it is bad to use a broomstick at night because it chases away the protective spirits who guard the home.

The cauldron

The cauldron is the vessel in which every storybook witch boils her obscure potions. Resembling a cooking pot, there are many legends surrounding the magic cauldron. Whether it is a source of abundance, a tool of torture as in Celtic myths, or a means of making people invincible as in the Greek legends, the cauldron has always been a container of transformation.

Salt

This important substance is sacred in almost every civilization. Its ability to preserve food and clean wounds makes it a symbol of purity. The fact that salt never perishes means that it embodies eternal life, but if it's scattered over soil, it turns the land infertile and is therefore associated with death. The alchemical symbol of salt (⊖) represents this duality, but also its protective powers.

The crystal ball

A seemingly impossible combination of solidity and translucency, the crystal ball acts as a window between the visible and invisible worlds. Legend has it each crystal ball is made from a part of the divine throne that shattered as it fell to Earth. Crystal has long been seen as a material that humans cannot control.

Candles

The German mystic Novalis once said that "in a candle's flame all of the forces of nature are active." The four elements, embodied by wax, wick, fire, and air, are brought together in a unique upward movement. A symbol of the link between the material and spiritual worlds, candles are used in many religious rituals, but also in magical practice. According to legend, candles should never be blown out, but put out with two wet fingers or smothered by means of a snuffer.

The Sabbath

The witches' Sabbath is not to be confused with the Sabbath celebrated as a "day of rest" by Jewish people every Saturday. At the same time, in the Judaic Book of Isaiah, the prophet strongly condemns a particular kind of "Sabbath," which he describes as a pagan festival linked to the lunar cycle. From here, it has long been associated with demonic festivities, during which witches ride around on their broomsticks.

The moon

The moon is important because it changes. It totally disappears from view for a few days a month, but it always returns, which is what makes it a symbol of death and rebirth. This cycle of eternal renewal and its successive phases also tie the moon to the rain, tides, vegetation, and fertility. Its complete cycle of 28 days matches the typical length of the menstrual cycle and so it is closely associated with women. It is an object of imagination, of dreams, of water and the cold (and the opposite of the sun). Considered the "female star," it sits at the edge of day and night, life and death, and is the symbol of Hecate and Artemis, which is why it is so strongly linked to witchcraft.

Tarot

Probably derived from 15th-century Italian card decks, the tarot is composed of 78 cards, the sum of the numbers one to twelve. The tarot is divided into "Major Arcana," of which there are 22 cards and no suits, and "Minor Arcana," of which there are 56 cards in four suits. The complex images on the cards give them great mystery. There are several ways to give a reading, but one of the most common is to draw five cards, which are then arranged in a cross shape, representing the past and future, hopes and goals, challenges and influences.

The spiral

A circular shape that is both open and progressive, the spiral embodies movement and optimism. It is associated with the permanence of being, but also change. The spirals found on shells link the shape to water, while its circularity connects it to the moon, both of which are connected to fertility.

The square

Even and regular, the square symbolizes order and stability. The symbol of perfection according to the mathematician Pythagoras, the square is calm and self-assured, the structure on which to build a home. It evokes the Earth and the permanence of being.

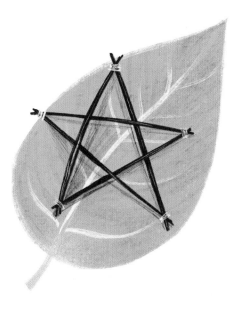

The pentagram

Based on the number five, the pentagram represents the union of unequal elements. When surrounded by a circle, the pentagram becomes the symbol of the pentacle, which is very significant to witches. When drawn into the air, it also represents the four cardinal points of earth, air, fire, and water, while the upward point represents the spirit.

The circle

The circle is a symbol of unity, completeness, the cycle of life and of rebirth, the sun and the sky. It is evidence of the richness in simplicity, and was perhaps the first form to be drawn by human beings. Its ability to enclose make it both a magical and protective symbol, which is where bracelets and rings derive their significance.

The triangle

The triangle shares the same symbolism as the number three, with its three harmonious and equal edges. Crucial to geometry and used as the base for calculating what is called the "golden ratio," it is probably the most mystical of all the geometric symbols. When pointing up, the triangle is a symbol for fire and the masculine; when pointing down, it represents water and women.

Practical Magic

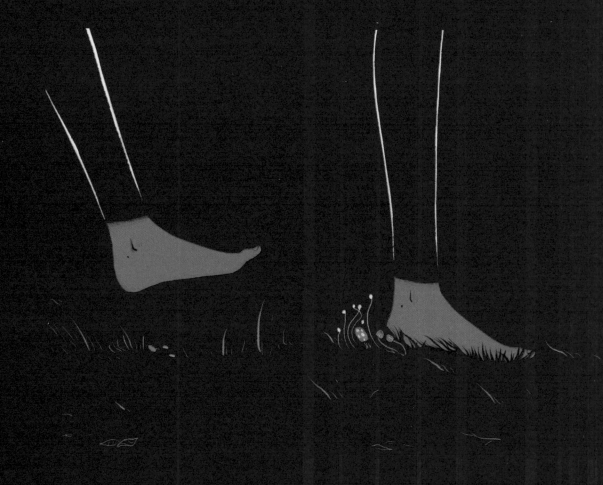

THE SECRET TO YOUR POWER IS in your mind. It is your knowledge, your capacity to reason, and the strength of your instincts that make you strong. Together these things help you to think, question, and feel. Never be fearful of using your abilities or rebelling if the situation demands it. Take the time to develop your senses—the first way we connect with the world. Remember that it is important to let your emotions run their course; learn to master them, but never suppress them, for they are your strength and not your weakness.

LASTLY, REMEMBER that you are a part of nature, that nature has an effect on you, and you on it. Over the following pages, you will find the keys to understand it better, the potions that will help you to care for others and the protective rituals that can bring peace and happiness.

The herbs
OF WITCHES

Here are a selection of important herbs whose magical properties have been celebrated since time immemorial. They are all easy to find and will be indispensable to your potion making.

Common sage

Since ancient times, sage has been an important herb to witches. Its Latin name *salvia* comes from *salvare*, meaning to cure or save.

MEDICINAL PROPERTIES: relieves period pains, digestive disorders, and night sweats; soothes ailments; treats throat infections.

MAGICAL PROPERTIES: purification (of places, objects, spirits) and protection, promotes clairvoyance and concentration.

USES: its leaves, whether fresh or dried, can be mixed in food, herbal tea, potions, and elixirs, or gathered in bundles and burned during purification rituals. When fresh, it can soothe insect bites.

FIND IT: in the garden; it's rare to find it in the wild. Harvest its leaves in the spring before it flowers, or in the autumn after flowering.

ASTRAL RELATION: Jupiter

Salvia Officinalis

Mentha x Piperita

Peppermint

Mint is an ancestral plant used for its invigorating properties. It has many varieties with sought-after medicinal and magical properties, including peppermint.

MEDICINAL PROPERTIES: relieves digestive disorders, eases pain, helps fight respiratory infections (colds, bronchitis, etc.).

MAGICAL PROPERTIES: protection, purification, prosperity, travel.

USES: its leaves, whether fresh or dried, are used in herbal teas and macerations, potions and elixirs. Its fresh leaves when carried bring prosperity.

FIND IT: in the garden. Harvest its leaves in spring and summer, ideally in the morning.

ASTRAL RELATION: Mercury

Bay tree

In ancient Greece, bay leaves were used by the Sibyls for apparitions. A shrub that can live for almost 100 years, the bay tree is a symbol of triumph and peace. It is used in both the kitchen and as part of winter solstice rites.

MEDICINAL PROPERTIES: with antibacterial powers, it stimulates the immune system, relieves indigestion, heals mouth ulcers, and eases joint pain.

MAGICAL PROPERTIES: protection, strength, luck, imagination. When a bay leaf is passed over a sheet of paper, it provides inspiration for those trying to write. Promotes successful divination.

USES: its leaves when dried can be given through meals, herbal tea, essential oil, macerations, or in potions and elixirs. It can also be carried in an amulet. Its berries can be turned into an oil that treats joint pains, or used to make Aleppo soap.

FIND IT: in the garden, its leaves can be harvested all year long.

ASTRAL RELATION: the Sun

Laurus Nobilis

Valerian

Valerian, whose Latin name means "doing well," has long been known to help people sleep. It's also popular with cats, because its roots give off an odor that cats love.

MEDICINAL PROPERTIES: helps fight insomnia, depression, exhaustion, stress and overwork, soothes muscle tension.

MAGICAL PROPERTIES: its roots, when dried and carried in an amulet or small silk bag, bring love and serenity.

USES: its dried roots can be used in herbal teas, essential oils, in potions and elixirs.

FIND IT: in the wild, on the edges of wetlands, but also in gardens. Its roots are harvested in autumn.

ASTRAL RELATION: Saturn

Valeriana Officinalis

Potions

Although knowing about plants and their virtues is important, your potions do not need to be complex in order to be effective. You can combine herbs to create a "synergy," or use them individually; it is your precision and intention that will make the difference. Once you have a recipe in mind, take time to connect with the energies of your chosen plants. Focus your intentions on them and prepare your potion using a ritual of your own devising. You might light a candle or burn incense, recite something written, sing, or even invent your very own incantation. To increase their power, you can also "charge" your potions with solar or lunar energy, by placing them for four hours under a hot sun or in moonlight.

The POWER of stones

STONES derive from the very bowels of the Earth. Shaped by time and the forces of nature, they are full of beneficial energies. Crystals, rough and polished stones, or even fossilized organic substances, such as amber, are grouped together under the term "gems." Each gem has its own energy, which is linked to its chemical composition, color, and shape. Depending on their desired effect: you can wear them in jewelry, carry them with you in your pockets, or display them at home. Some stones soothe, others promote communication or protection: learning their abilities will help you enormously. On this page, you will find a small selection, but always use your intuition when selecting stones.

Stones emit and receive energy, but over time they can become saturated. To continue enjoying their benefits, you must recharge them once a month. This can be done using the light of the sun or the moon, but the nature of your gem will determine which is better. Place your gem on the windowsill, for either a whole night of moonlight or for a few hours of sunlight. Another technique is to place your stone in a crystal geode, a kind of universal charger suitable for both solar and lunar gems.

Clean your gems

THE STONE you hold between your hands has come a long way since it was pulled out the ground. It is therefore recommended that you purify it in order to cleanse it of any stray energy. The most common method is to soak your stones in spring water for a few hours. You can then rinse them with clean water and before harnessing their power.

Tiger's eye

COLORS: stripes of golden yellow and brown
SYMBOLISM: instinct, courage
PROPERTIES: releases internal blockages and stress, and helps concentration. Tiger's eye is said to be a powerful shield against danger. It promotes decision making and good relationships with others; it stimulates the will, calms fears, and restores confidence.
ASTRAL RELATION: the Sun
RECHARGE: sunlight

Amber

COLORS: commonly yellow or brown, but more rarely green or white.

SYMBOLISM: purity, immortality

PROPERTIES: gives strength, purifies energy and helps people to assert themselves or express their personality. It is also said to relieve dental pain, and when placed near the bed, it promotes rest and fights against nightmares.

ASTRAL RELATION: the sun

RECHARGE: sunlight

Rose quartz

COLORS: pink or peach

SYMBOLISM: love, serenity

PROPERTIES: consoles and soothes, reassures and strengthens self-confidence. Rose quartz also brings calm and sweetness. Placed near the bed it promotes pleasant dreams.

ASTRAL RELATION: Venus

CHARGE: moonlight

Aventurine

COLORS: green, blue, red, or orange

SYMBOLISM: spirituality, knowledge

PROPERTIES: a stone of peace and balance, it absorbs negative energy, promotes creativity, brings clarity to ideas, and helps you to keep your cool.

ASTRAL RELATION: Venus

CHARGE: sunlight or moonlight

Labradorite

COLORS: a blend of gray, green, and blue

SYMBOLISM: regeneration, balance

PROPERTIES: as both a shield and a sponge, it absorbs negative energies and offers mental and emotional protections. Labradorite also helps to regain energy when tired, promote inspiration, and soothe anxieties.

ASTRAL RELATION: Mercury

CHARGE: sunlight

Amethyst

COLORS: pale mauve to deep violet

SYMBOLISM: wisdom, power

PROPERTIES: promotes concentration, intuition, and creativity. It helps against negative emotions and insomnia; it also soothes and promotes inner peace and openness to others.

ASTRAL RELATION: Jupiter

CHARGE: moonlight

How to use A CRYSTAL pendulum

A SMALL WEIGHT suspended by a wire, the pendulum is often used in divination. Its power is based on a practice known as "dowsing," which is thought to pick up on sensitivities and energy emitted by different bodies. In the past, along with the dowsing stick, it was used to locate sources of water. When its oscillating movements are interpreted, it can also be used to help find lost objects and to respond to questions.

A useful tool for learning more about yourself and your environment, the pendulum is a bridge between the world and our unconscious as it can help us understand messages that are not immediately clear. Translating its movements will also help you to develop your powers of intuition.

Most often these pendulums are made of crystal, but they can also be made of wood, glass, metal, and cut from different stones. Their shape also varies. Since the pendulum both transmits the energies of the universe to you and absorbs your energy in turn, choose the one that immediately attracts you the most.

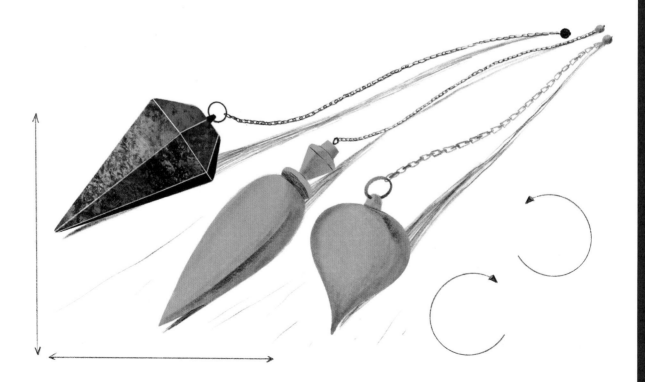

Make your own pendulum

THIS IS A POSITIVE TASK and taking care over making your pendulum will transmit positive energy into it. The two main components of the pendulum are the pendant and the cord. For the pendant, there are no rules: you can use a pebble, a gem, a ring, a piece of wood, or even a pearl. The pendulum is an extension of your consciousness, so the most important thing is to choose a material that inspires or is important to you.

The same goes for the cord: you might use a chain or a piece of string, but the more meaningful the material, the better. You do need to check that the cord will be strong enough to support the weight of your pendant and it shouldn't be longer than 8 inches. Assembly depends on the materials you use: you might need to make a hole in the pendant in order to attach it to the cord, or you might be able to use thin wire to hold the pendant in place.

Once your pendulum is created, wear it as much as you can so that it absorbs your energy. You can also charge it by leaving it in the sun or in moonlight, depending on its material.

How to use your pendant

TO GET TO KNOW YOUR PENDULUM, you need to hold it in your hands. Begin by pinching the cord between the thumb and forefinger of your writing hand. You can point your fingers at the floor, or have your hand parallel to the floor, whichever position works best for you. The most important thing is to be able to adjust the length of the cord, but without straightening your arm. Move the pendulum up and down by shortening and lengthening its cord until it stops swinging and starts moving in a circular motion. You have now found its ideal length.

You need to understand your pendulum's movements in order to read it. There are typically four answers which correspond to four movements:
- yes / true: rotates clockwise
- no / false: rotates anticlockwise
- I don't know: no rotation, but swinging from left to right
- I do not wish to answer: motionless

However, each pendulum can have its own behaviors, hence the importance of getting to know your own. Start by asking it simple questions that you already know the answer to, such as having it confirm your first name. Once you and your pendulum are calibrated, you will be able to start using it. Keep in mind that reading a pendulum is an exercise in patience, concentration, meditation, and connection.

Talismans, PENTACLES, and Amulets

SYMBOLS CAN HOLD GREAT POWER. Talismans are the embodiment of magic symbols, so to make one you must first choose the right symbol. The pentacle, which typically has the shape of a pentagram, is full of hidden meaning and is an example of a talisman. The pentagram's five-pointed star is enclosed in a circle, and is a force for good when its point is directed upward.

But there are many other auspicious talismans. For example, there are some that present the image of a "magic square," which is a grid that contains numbers adding up to the same total whether added horizontally, vertically, or diagonally.

Amulets

UNLIKE TALISMANS, amulets are objects
that you can charge with power. They can
be made of semiprecious stones, pebbles,
a feather, or a seashell. They don't even
need to come from nature; they can be
whatever object you like or care about, for
one reason or another. You might wear
your amulet around your neck or wrist, or
slip it into a small bag made of a fabric of
your choosing.

· ∧VENUS ↗   ∧ SUN ↗   ∧ SATURN ∧

∧ MERCURY ∧   ∧ MARS ∧   ∧ MOON ↗   ∧ JUPITER ∧

◇◇

Magic square

HENRI CORNEILLE AGRIPPA, a German magician of the 16th century, related magic squares to the seven planets and their seals that were known at the time. They are also sometimes called *kamea*, which means "lucky charm" in Hebrew.

In its simplest form, a magic square consists of nine boxes, with the sum of each line being equal, whether calculated horizontally, vertically, or diagonally. Traces of magic squares, which symbolize the harmony of our universe, have been founded in civilizations across history, with the first recorded one being traced back 3,000 years.

◇◇

4	9	2
3	5	7
8	1	6

Make your own talisman

TO BEGIN, take a piece of paper and colored pens that match the color of a planet of your choice (see table of properties below). Choose a quiet place, where you feel good, and light two candles. You might want to purify the space first, which you can do by burning sage or incense. Sit comfortably, calm your mind, and free it from worries, by focusing your breathing and closing your eyes. Take your time—nothing important has ever been done in a rush.

On your piece of paper, draw a large circle that represents the universe, then draw a smaller circle inside to represent yourself. At the top, between the two circles, trace a planetary seal of your choice. Then trace a five-pointed star inside the small circle. At the bottom, between the two circles, write your wish, or a word that corresponds to what you are missing. Then write your name or draw a symbol that characterizes you inside the star. Finally, draw a magic square on the other side: it can be one that corresponds to the planetary seal drawn on the front, or that of another planet.

To give your talisman energy, grasp it between two fingers, place it for a few moments above the flame of the candles, and scent it with incense while reciting an incantation of your choosing. The incantation could be a personal mantra, a poem, or song lyrics—what matters is its significance to you.

Carry this talisman with you for as long as you need to. When it's no longer required, do not throw it away, but burn it before scattering its ashes in a stream.

Table of properties

SUN	GOLD	YELLOW
MOON	SILVER	WHITE
VENUS	COPPER	GREEN
MERCURY	MERCURY	ORANGE
MARS	IRON	RED
JUPITER	TIN	BLUE
SATURN	LEAD	BLACK